Shoot Your Shot

By Eric Santos

Tables of Contents:

Preface:

Hello there! So glad to have you joining me. My name is Eric Santos and I am a 29-year-old entrepreneur and writer. I am a co-founder of a growing tech startup called Benchmark Intelligence, and I'm also the current owner of several other brands including SmellDope.com and Argosy Clothing. I am a published writer and the two niches I focus on deal with entrepreneurship/business and dating, Yes, I know, it's an odd combination, but as you read through this book, you'll notice there are definitely some great parallels you can make between the two fields.

I've been published by some illustrious publications including Business Insider, AskMen.com, Elite Daily, Yahoo Finance, Venture Beat, and many more. I have written several dating blog posts that have received millions of views. Although I am no stranger to having my content shared and read by many, this is my first book, and I am genuinely honored and proud that you've chosen to read it.

Although I started this preface with a humble brag, well really just bragging in general, the reality is I'm a pretty average guy. I wasn't born into any circle of wealth or influence. I was the first in my family to go to college and graduate. Everything I've obtained in my life, I've worked very hard for. I stand at a very average height of 5'8, and weigh about 155 pounds; I wear glasses and I am no male model by any means. I am a very average guy who has happened to accomplish some impressive feats. If you want to learn more about me, follow me on Instagram @ericsantosceo.

I wrote this book for the purpose of teaching men how to meet girls (aka shooting your shot) in this current digital era of sliding in the DMs and swiping right. If you're single and you don't know what either of those things mean, don't worry because this book will teach you what you need to know. This book is not a blueprint on how to be a pickup artist, and honestly, I find the idea of a pickup artist and their use of manipulation and trickery to meet women pretty weird and creepy.

I am going to cover some very straightforward and direct (but always respectful) ways that you can shoot your shot and meet women on social media, dating apps, and of course the old-fashioned way, in person. So whether you're newly single like my friends you're about to encounter in this book, or you've been playing the field for a while, I hope you find this journey helpful towards either finding your potential soulmate or just some great girls. Saddle up, boys, you're about to learn how to shoot your shot, accurately of course.

Chapter 1: The Current Dating Landscape

In the past year, I've had three very close male friends get divorced or opt out of long-term relationships (8+ years). All of three of them had met their significant others in high school or early years of college. These gentleman, ages 28, 29 and 31 all now had to learn how to be single for the first time in almost a decade. However, the dating landscape has since changed dramatically from the time when they were unattached.

Ten years ago, there were already well-established online dating services such as Match.com and eharmony, but there were no services such as Tinder or Bumble where users could make a decision over whether or not they found you attractive in seconds by simply looking at your pictures and swiping left or right.

Ten years ago, it wasn't unheard of to meet someone on social media (Myspace and early Facebook), but the term "slide in the DMs" was non-existent and the social media platforms of the times weren't nearly as focused on photos, selfies, and flexing like the Instagram and Snapchat of today. These newer social media platforms have created a culture where aesthetics have become more important than what you have to say. Social media, just like online dating, has dramatically changed over the last decade.

Consistent with how online dating has changed, social media has had a direct impact on the way people meet in traditional settings such bars, gym, coffee shops and so on. Nowadays, when you meet someone in person, many times it's more common to exchange Instagram handles in place of phone numbers. Also, due to the existence and popularity of these apps. you're actually less likely to meet someone in person because the accessibility of these apps has made many people lazier and less social. Yes, I too realize the irony of social media making people less social one download at a time.

Now, going back to the experience with my friends. During the last ten years, I've been single about eight of them in aggregate. Given my veteran experience being single (or alone, if you tend to look at the glass half empty) and my success as a published dating writer, I was my friends' main resource on acclimating to the single life in the current Tinder and Instagram age. It's funny because I never realized how much the dating landscape had changed until my newly single friends made the observation. Given that I've been single the majority of my adult life, I've never had to step away from the game for long periods of time with the exception of my last relationship which lasted a little less than year

Because I haven't stepped away from dating for a very long period of time, I never really noticed how much it'd changed until I had to help my friends acclimate to this much different dating climate. A climate I've always managed to keep up with without realizing it. When you're always looking at something and rarely step away from it, it's a lot harder to see the changes because they happen so slowly.

However, after some self-reflection in preparation for writing this book, I realized how much the dating landscape had changed over the last decade, even for me. In 2008-2010, all of the girls I'd met came as the result of in-person interactions, with the exception of one girl who I met on Myspace, and we dated briefly. Fast forward a decade, it's probably an even 50/50 split in terms of me meeting girls in person versus through apps/digital means. Even meeting my previously mentioned ex-girlfriend came as a result of the beautiful things that can happen from sliding in the DMs.

I am not alone in this regard either; the world is changing. According to dating app Zoosk, there are 40 million Americans using dating applications. This number doesn't even include the individuals who use non-dating specific apps such as Instagram and Facebook to meet people as well. There are not accurate metrics on the number of individuals who meet on non-specific dating apps, but it's safe to say that the number of individuals who meet other people online in America is definitely greater than 40 million.

We're certainly living in a digital world. As a founder of a technology company, I can tell you first-hand how technology makes our lives better and easier. Also, as a technology executive, I can also tell you that, many times, these technological improvements come at a price and with a few negative side effects. And the way that online dating and social media apps have changed how we meet people is no exception to the rule that technology helps and hurts at the same time.

Let's start with the positives. First and foremost, like most things disrupted by technology, dating and social media apps make meeting people extremely effective and easy. Compared to the old-fashioned way, specifically trying to meet someone at a bar, apps take much less time and money. Instead of hanging out at a bar on a Friday night for a few hours and buying a few drinks, trying to get a date for Saturday night, from the comfort of your home you can easily match with a someone on Tinder on Friday morning and have a date with her that same night or slide in a girl's DMs on a Tuesday, asking to grab a drink on the upcoming weekend.

Also, meeting people through apps allows you to connect with some great girls you may never have had the chance to meet otherwise. On Tinder, you can match with a girl who doesn't go out or frequent the same places (bars, gyms, etc.) that you do. Without Tinder providing the medium for you two to meet, that interaction probably would have never otherwise come to fruition. And let's be honest, even for the majority of guys who see a really pretty girl in person they'd like to talk to, they'd still prefer to match with her on Tinder or talk to her on Instagram. Who can blame them? Technology makes meeting people so much easier and stress-free.

With the type of accessibility that dating and social apps provide, naturally this comes with some difficulties. As a single guy utilizing these apps, you now have access to an almost endless number of girls you could potentially meet. With that being said, ladies now have just the same endless stream of options. Technically speaking, women have more options than men because there are more men than women on these apps (go figure).

Before dating and social apps, if you saw a very beautiful woman and had the courage to politely and confidently approach her and ask her on a date, you'd have a 90% better chance than any other guy because the other nine out of ten guys would not have the balls to try to talk to her. However, now with the availability of dating apps and social media, every guy is shooting their shot. The sad truth is, though, the majority of them are doing it wrong. The much sadder truth is that because these apps allow one to hide behind a screen when sending a message, there are some guys out there who send super rude and distasteful messages to girls, especially if they feel they are being rejected. These guys are jerks with no confidence and give respectful guys a bad name.

Whether you believe the pros outweigh the cons, or vice versa, technology has genuinely disrupted the way people date and meet others. The majority of dating literature out there doesn't reflect the dramatic paradigm shift that has occurred over the last decade. This book was created with the intention of helping guys respectfully meet girls in this ever-evolving digital age.

Chapter 2: Dating is a lot like Sales and Making Sales is Good

I have an interesting take on dating given my occupation. I'm the CEO of a software company that sells software to the retail and financial sector. One of my main responsibilities as a CEO is growing the company, aka sales. For the first two years, I did 100% of our sales myself. Before starting my company, I had a career in sales and account management at a large software company that did over $100M in annual sales.

Long story short, I'm pretty well-versed in sales. However, I haven't always been this way. Growing up, I was your typical introvert. Not only was I an introvert but I had extremely low self-esteem. I was a scrawny, buck-toothed Mexican kid with a heart of gold but not a lot of balls. True story, I didn't experience my first kiss until the age of 18 years old. Also, funny but true story, I received my first kiss and lost my virginity at the same time. I had no clue what I was doing! It is safe to say I was definitely a late bloomer.

I didn't start building self-confidence until I got to college. There were a number of factors that attributed to this, including losing my virginity, starting to work out, making new friends, and most importantly, finally understanding what I was capable of intellectually and physically.

I did alright in high school; I was a slightly above average student though I had little drive. I hung out with a few bad apples so that didn't help either. After high school, I went to junior college for two years before transferring to a four-year university to study business with an emphasis in entrepreneurship. While attending university, I met a lot of cool, competitive individuals who really helped me come out of introverted shell.

After college, I began working for the large software company I'd mentioned earlier. For the first two years, I held some entry-level, non-sales-related titles, and it wasn't until my third year there I was promoted into a more senior sales role. I was absolutely terrified, although by this time I was almost a different person than the scared little boy I was in high school. I was then, and still am to this day, an introvert. I remember telling my manager at the time, "I'm not sure if I'm cut out for sales; I'm not a very commanding or pushy person." This was where he helped me realized one of the biggest misconceptions I'd ever had, one that could have cost me everything I have today had I not learned it then. Before I tell you what this misconception is, close your eyes and take a second to think of the first adjectives that come to your mind when you think of salespeople. They are probably words like "shady," "aggressive," "pushy," and so on.

What my manager taught me was that although there are definitely shady sales people out there, the most successful sales people are just really good at helping people. Sales is not a game where there is a predator and there is prey. Sales is just the process of working with someone to see if your product/service could make the person's life easier. When you do sales right, you don't have to convince anyone to do anything; you're just providing them the facts in the easiest and most digestible way possible so that they can make the decision themselves whether they'd like to engage with your or your company.

Great sales people are honest and transparent, and the last thing they want to do is sell someone a product that won't provide any value. When I pitch my software to a president of a company and it helps her grow the company's revenue, it makes her life easier. I will always do my best to be honest with an organization; if I don't think our software is a fit after learning more about their needs and wants, I'll tell them we're not the best fit, even if they are willing to purchase it. Obviously, I am, like any other good sales person, also motivated by the monetary gains that I make in commission from closing deals, but I would never want to sell something that doesn't help the person I'm selling it to.

Now that we've framed sales as something that helps people and not something shady, let's talk about how dating is a lot like sales.

Take nothing personal

If you've ever been in sales before, you get really good at taking rejection. Rejection is quite frankly the hardest thing about sales. Sound familiar? It should because rejection is quite frankly the hardest thing about dating as well. Most people don't shoot their shot or ask out that girl they really like because they fear rejection. Even for the many brave souls who do shoot their shot, many times their attempt will come off as unconfident or shaky due to their internal fear of being rejected.

Do you know why most effective sales people are great at taking rejection? Two fundamental reasons: The first and more obvious reason is that they have a strong confidence in themselves and the product/service they are pitching. The second and probably more important reason is that somewhere along the way, they learned not to take rejection personally.

Rejection comes in various forms but it's important, regardless which form it comes in, not to take it personally. To best illustrate this, let me explain a concept in sales called a funnel. The definition of the sales funnel refers to the buying process that companies lead customers through when purchasing products. A sales funnel is divided into several steps, which differ depending on the particular sales model. This pretty much means the step involved in turning a stranger into a customer.

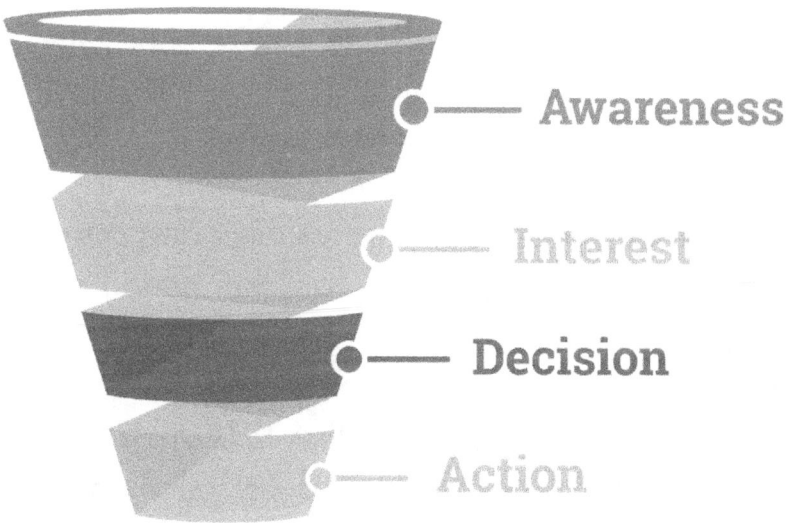

Awareness

Interest

Decision

Action

Each step along the funnel is a potential place to get rejected by the prospect. Let's say you never get past the awareness stage; this means you keep calling the prospect and they decide they don't even want to hear you out and only answer the phone once to finally tell you to leave them alone. In this case, the prospect is not even giving you the opportunity to tell them about the value your product or service provides. Although it may suck to get hung up on up to a hundred times a day, a good sales person doesn't take this type of rejection personally because they realize it's the prospect's loss on deciding against at least hearing out the solution that could potentially help them.

Let's say this same sales person is able to get another prospect on the phone and they show heavy interest. The prospect even agrees to sit down for a product demonstration and the initial reception is super positive. One week after this product demonstration and even further research on the behalf of the prospect, they decide they don't want to buy the product. Although the rejection may sting a little given the prospect was very close to buying, the sales person doesn't take this rejection personally because he or she realizes they did their best at trying to articulate how the product could provide value, but the truth is the product wasn't a match for this specific person's needs. That doesn't mean the product sucks or isn't appealing to others; it just means this product isn't for this specific person. A great salesperson will feel content when this revelation is made because it prevents both parties from wasting further time.

Now let's apply the above examples to dealing with rejection when it comes to dating. Let's say you approach a woman at the bar or maybe you slide in the DMs of some woman that you recently started following. In the bar example, you politely ask her if you can buy her a drink and she declines your offer. In the Instagram scenario, you send a DM asking if you can take her out sometime and she replies no.

Normally, being shot down like in the examples above can prove disheartening but it shouldn't be if you don't take it personally. In both scenarios, the woman didn't give you a chance to get to know her or tell her anything about yourself. There is nothing wrong with that; you approached her and she has every right to decline your advancements. With that being said, she made a decision after a few seconds of looking at you or your Instagram profile and decided to say no. You shouldn't take that personally because the decision to not talk to you wasn't personal; she doesn't know you. Also, you don't know her back story, so maybe she's currently talking to someone or perhaps she just had a really bad day. Either way, anytime someone rejects your initial advancement, just smile, tell her to have a great night, and walk away.

Now let's say your initial attempt at the bar or on Instagram was successful and you are able take her on a date. In your eyes, the date went great, conversation flowed easily, and you really enjoyed her company. A few days later, you text her asking to take her out again, but she doesn't reply. You try a few days later and she hits you with a "Thank you very much for the dinner but I just wasn't feeling it enough to go out again." Ouch! That hurts a lot more than if it was a quick "no" at the bar. However, just like before, you still shouldn't take it personally. Although the rejection was much more personable because you had an initial connection, the rejection itself wasn't personal because it wasn't about you, it was about her.

You may have enjoyed the date and maybe she did too but that's not always enough. Her requirements, as quantified as they may be, were not met for a second date. You put your best foot forward and did your best to sell yourself, but she ultimately decided not to purchase what you were selling, not because anything was wrong with you; you just may not be the most compatible fit for her.

An easy analogy to understand is imagining yourself as a beautiful ZL1 convertible Camaro. She was considering purchasing you but realized it snows 50% of the year where she lives and is probably better off with something like an AWD Honda CRV. Just because she'd rather go with another car doesn't mean anything is wrong with you; you're still a 650hp badass, but you're just meant for other drivers.

Remember, confident men don't take rejection personally, and they are always polite even during rejection. Unconfident jerks take rejection like a punch in the face and thus respond rudely like the losers they are. Don't be an unconfident jerk.

Persistence pays off, but it can also cost you

A good sales person always follows up; however, a great sales person knows exactly when to follow up. When it comes to sales, the follow-up is super important because almost nothing is sold on the first shot. According to the business research firm, Sirius decisions, it takes a sales person eight cold call attempts before they reach a prospect, meaning they have to call someone eight times before they even get a chance to speak with them. However, even after you get that initial meeting with them, 80% of sales require five follow-up calls after the meeting (according to marketingdonut). This means that a typical sale requires 13 calls and one meeting on average to close a deal.

So, what does this have to do with dating? Are you saying that you need to send eight unanswered messages to a girl on Instagram or Tinder before she replies? No, I'd actually suggest against that, though one or two follow-ups won't hurt. The sales follow-up metrics I shared do not apply to dating; dating should require a fraction of the number of follow-ups that sales do.

The main point here is when it comes to dating, just like sales, the right amount of follow-up and persistence really pays off. Girls appreciate a guy who shows persistence and a real effort to get to know them, the same way prospects do in sales. Follow-ups are also important because many times when you shoot your shot and it misses, it may not be because the girl isn't interested. Take Tinder for an example: You match with a beautiful girl, send her a message and never hear from her. You give up because you think maybe she swiped right on you by accident. The reality is that she likely got another 50 matches that day and your message got pushed down to the bottom of her inbox and she never read it. But let's say you followed up at least once like you should have; your message would have ended up on top and she would have read it, and just maybe, you guys eventually would date and live together happily ever after (if you're into that kind of thing).

However, just like in sales, you can definitely be too persistent. In sales, this results in companies blacklisting and blocking your email and phone number from reaching out to them. In dating, the side effects of being persistent range from being blocked to public shaming (sharing screenshots of your attempts) to much more serious consequences such as police involvement and/or restraining orders. So, although it pays off to be consistent, it can certainly hurt you. My rule of thumb is if you're considering whether your attempt is one too many, you should definitely not do it. Respect is key when following up. Over the next few chapters, I'm going to go over how you can respectfully be persistent on Instagram, Tinder, and in person. During the last chapter, we will revisit this again in more detail.

Chapter 3: Sliding in the DMs

It's hard to believe but social media has been around for two decades now, maybe even longer depending what you consider the first social platform. Although social media was originally created as a way to connect online with friends and family, social media's dating utility has always been a driver of its growth. Dating was a part of social media at its inception when it was created twenty years ago; however, dating has never been more engraved into the culture of social media than today and that's largely attributed to the advent of Instagram.

Instagram was founded in late 2010 by Kevin Systrom and Mike Krieger, created as a cool way to share photos with friends and family. Up until this point, sharing digital media such as photos on social media sites like Facebook and Twitter was common, but Instagram was the first big social media platform to focus on photos exclusively. At this point, social media had changed forever because, almost overnight, how you looked became more important than what you had to say.

Instagram was acquired by Facebook in 2012 for a cool one billion dollars. No bad for two years' worth of work, right? Many critics and analysts thought Facebook greatly overpaid for the young social media platform, but fast-forward six years and it's easy to see how smart of an investment this had been. Instagram is currently on track this year (2018) to generate eight billion dollars in ad revenue and has currently surpassed one billion users. Yup, you read that right, one billion users, and you can bet your pretty penny a few hundred million of these users are single.

In December 2013, Instagram launched the direct message feature, around the same time the phrase "Slide in the DMs" was coined. People could still meet on Instagram prior to this, but you could only have a conversation with someone through their comments for the whole public to see. The direct message feature gave you the opportunity to shoot your shot to your favorite Instagram model and be rejected behind closed doors.

Unlike applications that are made specifically for dating like Tinder and Bumble, there are not a whole lot of metrics regarding direct messaging and relationships formed via Instagram. However, I can anecdotally tell you that the number is high because my last and most serious relationship came to fruition from an Instagram DM, and I have a number of friends who've dated people they've met on Instagram.

Many singles prefer meeting people through Instagram over dating apps because it doesn't feel as contrived.

Although it's uncommon for celebrities to use dating apps, it's super common for them to slide in the DMs of attractive followers. Even singer Nick Jonas admits in the past to sliding in the DMs and being left on read (when the receiver doesn't respond to the DM but reads it). Don't feel too bad for Nick, he eventually found his current wife, Priyanka Chopra, by sliding in the DMs (but this time on Twitter).

Now before you start getting your Nick Jonas on and sliding in the DMs unsolicited, let's go over some things you can do first to increase your odds.

Profile Optimization

If you think about the task of sliding in the DMs as applying for a job, your Instagram profile is definitely your resume. Heck, it's probably more important than that — it's your portfolio. Your Instagram profile is going to be the first thing someone sees when you follow them or like their photo. Also, if you slide in someone's DMs, you can sure be they will click your icon to give your profile a glance. I use the word glance purposely because much like a resume, unless your profile stands out, they will only take a couple of seconds to look at it then move on. Your profile will set the first impression, so let's make it a good one.

Some people use their Instagram as a medium to post mirror selfies, while others post nothing but memes or motivational pictures (we all know those), and some use it as a place to flex their nice things. Although these are all legit reasons to use Instagram and everyone should be able to post what they want, ideally you should use Instagram as a way to document your life. This holds especially true if you plan on using Instagram as a way to meet people. When you're able to successfully document your life, it provides whoever follows you admission into your world and an opportunity to learn more about you.

This helps create relatability and lets people feel like they know you without really knowing you. They may see that you both workout at the same gym, dine at the same restaurants, or vacation in the same areas of the world. When you're able to create this relatability, people are more willing to meet you when you reach out to them because you're no longer a complete stranger, although in reality you are. It's already such a scary endeavor meeting strangers online; you can help put their mind at ease that you're a normal person with common interests.

As mentioned before, I truly believe people should be able to post whatever the heck they want on their Instagram. It's your form of self-expression and your profile should hold true to yourself. However, here are some dos and don'ts I'd suggest that can help optimize your profile if you're trying to meet someone on Instagram.

Don'ts:

- Avoid too many mirror selfies. Although it's completely normal to have pictures of just yourself, you don't want the majority of them to come in the form of a mirror selfie. If you want to post a photo of yourself, have someone take it for you or just use the self-timer on your phone. Mirror selfies come off a little more vain and they make people think you're by yourself all the time. Save the mirror selfies for your story.

- Having too many of the same type of picture or pictures shot at the same place. This especially holds true to my fitness folks. If you have an amazing physique, show it off. However, do your best to avoid having all your pictures featured at the gym; it may come off as if the gym/working out is your only interest in life.

- Over-filtered photos. Don't overuse the saturation in order to look tanner, or use filters that distort the photos.

- Posting cadence. This is something I struggle with personally but unless you're a social media influencer, don't post a picture every day (I'm talking about your timeline, not your story). Girls will definitely think you're into yourself. I personally think once a week is an ideal cadence. On the opposite end of the spectrum, don't post once every six months either. Sometimes meeting someone on Instagram isn't an overnight thing (however many times it is), so you'll want to post every once in a while to let them know you're still there. P.S. You're allowed to post on your story on a much higher cadence.

Dos:

- Document the cool things you do. If you're out of town for the weekend with your friends, snap a photo in this new setting. Yes, I totally understand that you should live in the moment and enjoy traveling, but it doesn't take anything away from the experience to take one minute to snap a photo that you'll have for memories.

- Framing is important. It's ideal if you can keep a consistent framing, such as making sure all of your photos are cropped in a 1x1 square format. With that being said, you should switch up how you are framed in that square. If you're showing off your shoes, you'll want your full body to be framed in the square. However sometimes you should switch it up and be closer framed, such as taking a photo from the waist up.

- Lightly edit/touch up your photos. Keyword here is *lightly.* You can really help add that magic touch to your photos by using an app like Lightroom or Presco. The main variables you should adjust are exposure, contrast, highlights, shadows, and sharpening.

- Use witty captions. Far too many people try to go the long motivational route when it comes to captions. Truth be told, funny/witty/punny captions go a longer way with the ladies. Plus, when it's time to use a longer more thought-provoking caption, the caption is more powerful because your timeline is not saturated with similar captions.

- Use your story for photos you're on the fence with. For those photos you're second-guessing about posting, such as another shirtless photo (even though your last photo was shirtless as well), just post them on your story. Everyone can see them for 24 hours, and if you feel so compelled after that, you can still post it on your timeline. However, posting to your story will help mitigate posting photos you may regret.

Leg work

Ok, your profile now looks badass, so it's time to slide in the DMs of the first beautiful girl you see, right? Well, we're not quite there yet. There is some leg work we need to do first.

Ideally, you don't want to send a completely unsolicited DM to someone without any interaction first. Let's say you stumble upon the profile of someone you're interested in on your explore feed; instead of sending them a DM right away, simply follow them and maybe like a photo or two first. In an ideal situation, they'll follow you back and even like a photo or two of yours. At this point, you'd probably be safe to shoot a DM (we'll go over the mechanics of this soon) or you can let it marinate for a while, which I'd recommend.

Let's now say you followed them and liked some photos but they didn't follow you back. Don't worry, this doesn't always mean they saw your profile and weren't interested. They may have missed the notification or were busy when they received the follow notification; this holds especially true if the person has a few thousand followers or more.

At this point, just be patient for a while and subtly let them know you're there. Check out their stories, and when they post a photo, like it, and if you're ever feeling so daring, comment on it. However, if you're going to comment, post something funny; don't post anything too direct in the comments. Another hack: If you're going to like a photo of theirs, don't do it in the first few hours of them posting as they will be flooded with notifications in the first few hours.

Ok, you've now been patient for a while and after some effort, you've failed at getting any sort of interaction (follows, likes, etc.) back from the person you're interested in. Don't worry! Not all hope is lost; you can still shoot your shot but understand it's going to be more of a Hail Mary than a quick route.

It's now time to make your stand, slide in the DMs, and shoot your shot. As cheesy as it sounds, sliding in the DMs is almost an art form. You're doing your best to get this person's attention, make them smile, avoid making them feel uncomfortable while you come off as confident, all at the same time. Hopefully you've interacted with this person so your message isn't such a "cold call." However, even if you were patient and didn't receive any interaction back, you can still be successful with your shot.

Story time

I am a strong believer in using a story post as an "in" to talking to the person you're interested in. Even if they have the function to reply to their story turned off, you can still send a DM using the message button and reference the story post.

There are two main types of DMs you can send: One method uses flattery, while the other uses comedy, though the best DMs have some sort of combination of both. The last thing you want to send is a simple, lame message such as, *"Hi"* or *"What's up?"* Here are some potential example DMs I'd suggest sending, depending on the type of story post referenced.

The first and most likely scenario you may encounter is a woman posting a selfie or photo of herself on her story. The best strategy on a selfie story post is to lead with a compliment. However, even when leaving a compliment, you want to be witty and use some creativeness. One of my favorite adjectives to use when making a compliment is *"ridiculously,"* such as *"you are ridiculously gorgeous,"* or *"Why are you so ridiculously attractive?"* You can also try a more comedic compliment such as, *"You have a really nice face,"* or *"You are so good looking it's almost strange."* These compliments seem a little silly, but they will stand out and potentially make her laugh and feel flattered at the same time which is your most ideal outcome when shooting your shot.

If you're not feeling so daring to shoot your shot right off the bat with a compliment, the second scenario of simply creating conversation based off what they are doing in their story may be more for you. An example of sparking conversation may look something like this: They post a picture of their lunch and it happens to be at one of your favorite spots, so you can reply with something like, *"You have such great taste, that's one of my favorite spots in town."* You can use this method to start conversation in order to get a reply first before shooting your shot.

Now it's time for action. Regardless of whether you lead with a compliment or simply start conversation by talking about something on their post, you will want to have a call to action within a few messages. Examples of calls to actions could be asking them for their number or asking them out. Remember, these are direct messages, so you need be direct.

When you make your call to action, be specific. NEVER ask to hang out sometime, but rather reference something specific like, *"May I take you to your favorite restaurant sometime?"* However, there is one last thing you will want to do before making that call to action and that's asking them if they are available/single. The flow of messages may look something like this:

You: *"Geez, you are ridiculously beautiful"* (in reply to her story selfie)

Her: *"Aww, thank you soo much :)"*

You: *"You're welcome. Do you live in _____? I feel like I've seen you before."*

Her: *"Yes, I do, how about you?"*

You: *"I do as well, Apologies for being so direct but are you single?"*

Her: *"Yes I am :) How about you?"*

You: *"Great, I am as well. May I take you to dinner sometime?"*

Her: *"Yes you may, here is my number xxx-xxx-xxxx."*

Here is one more example where you can start the conversation more casually and ask them if they are single and ask them out at the same time.

You: *"That looks sooo good, where is that from?"* (in reply to her pizza story post)

Her: *"It is! It's from _____"*

You: *"Thanks! I'm going to have to try it out sometime, my favorite pizza place is ___, they have an amazing Hawaiian pizza, have you ever been there?"*

Her: *"No I haven't but that sounds really good, I need to try it sometime!"*

You: *"You definitely do! So I have to ask, are you single? Lol If so, I'd love to take you there sometime. If you're not, he sure is a lucky guy lol."*

Her: *"HAHA yes I'm single as a pringle."*

You: *"So glad to hear that lol. Well, may I have your number, so we can arrange this sometime?"*

Her: *"Yeah for sure! It's xxx-xxx-xxxx."*

Keep in mind, the two above scenarios are real-life examples that have worked for me, but it may not go perfectly every time. Sometimes there is much more back and forth conversation before she is comfortable enough giving you her number or committing to meeting in person.

Being left on read

Sometimes you shoot your shot and it hits the net like water; sometimes you shoot your shot and you're left on read. This means you sent a message, she read it and decided not to reply. For the majority of men, they shoot their shot once, get left on read and their journey stops there. There is nothing wrong with this strategy per se because the last thing you want to do is harass someone with constant messages, but I'm a firm believer you should shoot your shot twice.

When you shoot your shot the first time, I'd say 75% of the time, her lack of response was completely intentional. Meaning, she read your message, retained it, took a glance at your profile and then decided not to reply. However, for the other 25% of the time, she might have been busy when she read the message or maybe she never read it at all because she was bombarded with messages from other dudes, leaving your message at the bottom of her Instagram inbox. She also could have read the message, but it was such a boring message she didn't even take the time to check out your profile.

For this reason, I am believer that you should always shoot your shot twice if needed. It's also a good practice to switch it up on the second attempt. Meaning, if you lead with a compliment on her appearance on the first message you send, make sure your second message is based on a conversational point regarding what she's doing and vice versa. It's always worth shooting the second shot and most girls appreciate the follow-up.

Now if you really want to be persistent, you can follow-up one more time if she hasn't responded but this is a little more of a risky attempt, and honestly, the more messages you send after the third message, the lower chance you have of getting a reply from each additional shot. My ex-girlfriend finally got back to me after my fourth message attempt, but I can tell you this is an outlier and something I don't normally suggest doing. You don't want to be one of those guys who is talking to himself in her DMs, the conversation thread consisting of seven messages from you and zero from her.

The last and probably most important thing I'd like you to retain from shooting your shot in her DMs is simply not to be a jerk. I see way too many screenshots of dudes who send a girl several DMs complimenting her and after not getting a reply, they decide to start sending rude messages filled with profanity. Sending someone messages and not receiving a reply is NEVER justification for being a jerk or saying something rude. Remember, you are sending these messages unsolicited, so you always want to be kind and respectful.

Chapter 4: Time to Swipe Right

Dating has changed dramatically since its inception. It once consisted of first date proposals and fathers making deals with other fathers about whom their daughters will marry. Over the next few centuries/ millennia, dating continued to evolve for the better but changed forever in 1995 with the advent of Match. com, the first dating website.

Match.com created the first medium online that people could use to meet other people romantically. Around this time, email and instant messaging began to flourish, allowing people to connect quickly and more conveniently. In 1998, the movie *You've Got Mail* became a box office hit and a classic, and it wasn't just a cute rom-com — it was the first major movement to semi normalize online dating.

Over the next few decades, the online dating industry continued to grow as well as the players in the space. After Match.com, came JDate, eHarmony, Plenty of Fish, and so on. Not only did the number of dating services increase but at no surprise, so did the number of individuals meeting other people online. In 1998, only 4% of Americans met their partners via online dating, while only a decade later, that number increased to 23%. That number is even higher now.

Dating, both online and conventional, experienced another dramatic shift in 2012 with the inception of the world's current most popular (depending on what metric you look at) dating application, Tinder. Before Tinder, the majority of online dating services such as Match.com and eHarmony focused their marketing efforts on targeting individuals looking to find their soulmate/ life partner. Although people used these sites (specifically Match.com) for casual dating/hooking up, the majority of their user base was looking for their potential wife/husband. This was very apparent in their user base, as right around the time Tinder came out, over 82% of Match.com's user base was over the age of 30.

The majority of singles in their 20s and early 30s were turned off by online dating at the time because they felt it was only for desperate people who were looking for a spouse but incapable of meeting someone through normal means (in person/public, through friends, etc.). Plus, the majority of the existing dating services had costly monthly subscriptions ($20 - $50 a month) and one-hundred-question questionnaires that users had to fill out if they hoped to find someone compatible; a combination of these points added more fuel to the narrative that online dating was for the desperate.

Tinder changed the game when it came out because it was the first online dating service that was agnostic in terms of intent, meaning you could use Tinder to hook up, find a girlfriend, find a friend with benefits, or look for your life partner. This and in combination with the fact that it was free and super easy to set up made it a hit with folks in their 20s and early 30s. Today, Tinder has over 50 million users worldwide with almost half of its user base falling between the ages of 25 and 34.

If you're reading this book, currently single, and not on Tinder (or maybe on the fence about it), I'd definitely suggest giving it a try if you're looking to actively date. For those who've never seen the inside of the Tinder app, it's pretty straightforward. Your profile only consists of two components: a couple of photos and your bio which has a five-hundred character limit. When you browse through profiles, you swipe left on the profiles you're not interested in and right on those who you are interested in. If you and someone mutually swipe right on each other, you are put into a conversation thread together where you can shoot your shot and get to know each other. It's pretty damn simple, although there are a lot of idiosyncrasies and variables that you need to know to be successful on the app.

The Profile

Much like your Instagram profile, when it comes to dating on Tinder, your profile is your resume/portfolio. However, your Tinder profile is much more limited in scope of what you can share (handful of photos with no captions versus hundreds of photos with captions), so you need to do a lot more with much less.

Let's go over your photos first. On Tinder, you can post up to nine photos, although I do not suggest using all nine photo spots because I just feel that's doing too much. On the opposite of the spectrum, I'd strongly suggest against only posting one or two photos. It's much harder to sell yourself with only one or two opportunities. The ideal range of photos you should share on your profile is somewhere around four to six photos. Also, much like your Instagram profile, these photos should vary in nature. Here are some tips on potential types of photos you should share and types of photos you should avoid.

Photos you should include:

- Portrait Shot. You should have at least one portrait shot on your profile that has your face clearly in it, but it shouldn't be a selfie shot. Also, make sure you smile in this portrait shot. Tinder shared a statistic with *Men's Health* that users are 14%

more likely to be swiped right if they're smiling, and 20% more likely to be swiped right if they're facing forward. You probably want this portrait shot to be the first photo you use on your profile; be sure to turn off Tinder's smart photo feature.

- One formal-ish photo. If you are dressed very casual in the majority of the photos, post one photo where you are dressed in formal attire; whether it's from a wedding or a holiday party, find one setting where you are dressed formally or at least business casual. This will show your potential matches that you clean up well. Also, on the opposite side of the spectrum, if you work in finance and all of your photos feature you dressed formally, make sure to have a photo or two of yourself in a t-shirt, jeans, or shorts so that you can let potential matches you know how to chill as well.

- An adventurous/traveling photo. If you ever have the opportunity to go somewhere cool or adventurous, whether it be Paris or the Grand Canyon, take a cool photo. Having a photo like this shows you're somewhat cultured and like exploring, a trait that many find attractive. One caveat: If you are at a very touristy location, try to avoid taking a very basic photo that your potential matches may have seen on other profiles.

- A photo doing what you love. You should have one photo of you doing what you love on your profile, assuming what you love doing is cool. So, if video games are your only passion, please don't post a picture of you playing. However, if you love hiking, basketball, boxing, bodybuilding, creating art, or whatever it may be, snap a cool photo of yourself in the act of doing what you love. Women find it quite attractive when a man is very passionate about something and work towards improving at it.

Photos you should avoid:

- Mirror selfies. Earlier, I'd mentioned how you should avoid having too many on your Instagram profile, but it doesn't hurt if you have a few for those times when you can't find anyone else to take a photo of you. However, if you're only sharing a handful of photos on your Tinder, NONE of them should be mirror selfies. You should even try to avoid non-mirror selfies (front-facing camera selfies). Just find someone to take five photos of you.

- Group photos. Avoid group photos of you and your friends. You don't want someone who's swiping on you to have to try and guess who you are. However, photos with your mom, grandma, dog are cute and cool to post.

- Photos of things. Avoid at all cost posting photos of things. I didn't even realize it was a trend for guys to post multiple photos of their trucks/cars until I had a female friend tell me it was quite common. Although some flexing is allowed on Instagram, I'd say stay away from flexing on Tinder.

Five-hundred characters of suave

Now that we have your photos in order, it's time to work on your bio, which is almost as important. I say almost because the fact is many people will swipe left or right on you without looking at your bio, but for those who might be on the fence and take a look at your bio, you'll want to make sure it seals the deal on the right swipe.

Tinder limits your bio to five-hundred characters. Some may feel this is a hindrance, but I feel this is a good thing; if you're not able to either make someone laugh or understand who you are in five-hundred characters, then you're probably not going to be able to do either with more words anyways. This character limit forces you to be concise and negates you from rambling too much.

Although I strongly suggest against not using a bio at all, when it comes to your bio, less is more and funnier is better. Some guys will use their bio to exclusively talk about themselves while other guys will simply use a funny quote as their bio. I suggest you go the route of talking about yourself but in a brief and amusing manner. There are ways to humble brag (if you happen to be so cool) on your bio in a low-key, funny way.

It's important to not take yourself to seriously in your bio even if you're a super cool and accomplished person. Avoid the cliché phrases such as saying you enjoy working out or hiking and believe me, everyone loves traveling, so don't even bother. You don't want to give away too much in the bio because many details are better learned over conversation.

Here are eight different types bios that you can use for inspiration.

This type of bio shows you have confidence by stating you are your city's most eligible 5'4 bachelor.

"(Your city)'s most eligible (height) bachelor."

Eric

🎓 California State University, Fresno

📍 less than a mile away

Fresno's most eligible 5'8.5 bachelor.

This type of bio is the day and night bio where you state what your occupation is during the day and a funny fact about a hobby during the night.

"9th grade teacher by day, semi-pretentious craft beer aficionado by night."

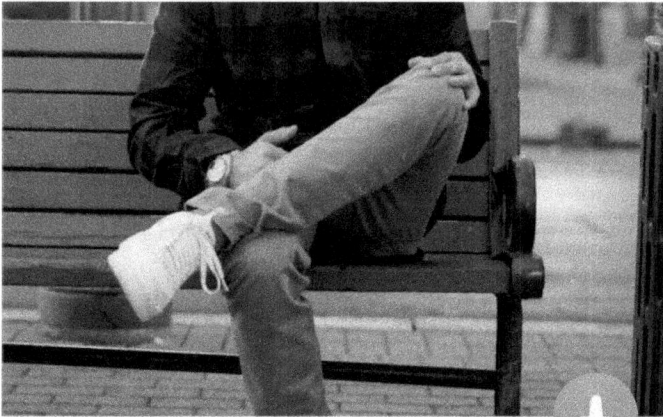

Eric

🎓 University of California, Los Angeles

📍 less than a mile away

9th grade teacher by day, semi-pretentious craft beer aficionado by night.

This example bio allows you to humble brag and state what you do for a living, followed by a funny fact and a question. You may get people swiping right on you just so they can tell you how to keep your plant alive.

"My name is ____, I'm an entrepreneur and I have a dying succulent plant. How do you keep one alive?"

Eric

🎓 University of Cincinnati

📍 less than a mile away

My name is Eric, I'm an entrepreneur and I have a dying succulent plant. How do you keep one alive?

This example is the good ol' three-point bio. Just share three completely random things about yourself. And hey, you can even get a little braggadocious.

"I wrote a book called "Shoot your shot".
I once backpacked around Lake
Tahoe in 13 days.
When I was eight, I broke my arm
flying a kite.
What about you?"

Eric

🎓 University of San Francisco
📍 less than a mile away

I wrote a book called "Shoot your shot".
I once backpacked around Lake Tahoe in 13 days.
When I was eight, I broke my arm flying a kite.

What about you?

The less than greater than bio is a fun way to state your preferences. List out sets of random things you have an opinion about and indicate which you think is best. And the more absurd or seemingly trivial, the better.

**"Sunday fundays > lazy Sundays
Skiing > snowboarding
Electric guitar < acoustic guitar (but
I play both)
Peanut butter > jelly (Though they still go
together pretty well. Maybe we will too.)"**

Eric

⌐ Stanford University

◎ less than a mile away

Sunday fundays > lazy Sundays
Skiing > snowboarding
Electric guitar < acoustic guitar (but I
play both)
Peanut butter > jelly (Though they still go
together pretty well. Maybe we will too.)

A pro vs con bio is a great way to humbly brag about yourselves in the pros and be funny/self-deprecating in the cons.

"Pros:

-I own my own business

-Cleans up well, makes a great +1

-Never been addicted to crack

Cons:

-Not Ryan Gosling

-Can and will serenade you to sleep

-My cookie recipe will definitely ruin your diet"

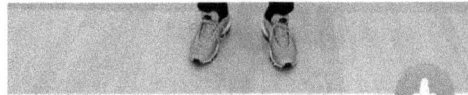

Eric

🎓 University of Colorado Boulder

📍 less than a mile away

Pros:
-I own my own business
-Cleans up well, makes a great +1
-Never been addicted to crack

Cons:
-Not Ryan Gosling
-Can and will serenade you to sleep
-My cookie recipe will definitely ruin your diet

This example bio is what I call a one-liner. Although it's not my favorite example on the list because it doesn't help your match learn anything about you (other than you're bad at everything), but I promise clever one-liners like this will make your match laugh. These types of bios are risky but work well if you choose the right one liner.

"I hear you like bad boys. I'm bad at everything."

Eric

💼 Sales at Solar City

◎ less than a mile away

I hear you like bad boys. I'm bad at everything.

The review bio. This example bio allows you to comedically brag about yourself in the third person via reviews you write yourself.

"What an amazing cook" - Guy Fieri
"The best dressed guy we know" - GQ
"I wish he was my personal trainer" - Hulk
"I'm glad I swiped right" - Future You

Eric

💼 CPA at Streamline CPA Solutions

◎ less than a mile away

"What an amazing cook" - Guy Fieri
"The best dressed guy we know" - GQ
"I wish he was my personal trainer" - Hulk
"I'm glad I swiped right" - Future You

Conversation Time

Ok, you now have a badass profile and everyone you swipe right on is swiping right back on you, right? Well, unless you are Ryan Gosling, not everyone you swipe right on will swipe right back on you and that's fine; it helps you save time and only focus on matches who are interested in you (unless they swiped right by accident). I personally don't have any cool strategy on swiping; I'd just say swipe right and cross your fingers.

When you do get a new match, it's a beautiful thing. A little red and white flame push notification blesses your phone screen. You almost drop your phone in excitement while opening the app to see who it was that swiped right on you because let's be honest, there may be times we swipe right even though we were on the fence, and other times when we are so swooned over them we make a prayer before we swipe right.

Now that you have the match, it's time to shoot your shot. Much like boxing, I'd suggest you take the center of the ring and shoot your shot first. However, if they message you first, no worries, as that's a good sign your profile worked. In any case, unless they messaged first or you're on Bumble, you should send the first message. Side note: all of the above tips I've laid out thus far for Tinder work for Bumble as well; I've just focused on Tinder due to the fact that it has a much larger user base.

Luckily for you, when you shoot your shot on Tinder, it's much easier than sliding in the DMs on Instagram because on Tinder, mutual interest has already been expressed while on Instagram, many times you're sending an unsolicited message. For this reason, you don't have to be as creative or daring as you do on Instagram, but with that being said, don't be lazy and start with "Hey," "Hi," or "What's up?"

The Opener

I'd suggest always leading with a compliment and introducing yourself. The same criteria I'd given on compliments in the Instagram chapter hold true when making a compliment on Tinder. Such as . . .

"Geez, you are ridiculously beautiful. Hello _____, my name is Eric, nice to meet you. . ."

This is not the completed message I'd suggest sending, but I'd like to go over this portion with you before going over the remainder of the message. First, as I'd suggested earlier, make compliments in a clever way. I spiced up this compliment by using "geez" and "ridiculously." This type of compliment is more personable and conversational, as if you were saying it in person.

Next, you'll want to say hello and use their name. This subtle detail is important because it shows your message is not just a copy-and-paste template you send every girl because you've addressed your match by name. The last portion is me introducing myself, which is pretty self-explanatory.

That's the introduction; now you can go one of two ways with the remainder of the message. You can either ask a question or make a call to action. The majority of time I'd suggest going down the question route because it doesn't come off as strong. When it comes to questions, it's great if you can ask a question related to something on their profile, such as a specific inquiry about a hobby, occupation, or their dog. If they don't give away too much information on their profile, just ask a general question about their life. You can ask them a very open-ended question to get a broader answer or a more specific question if there is a specific conversation point you'd like to talk about.

Below are some example messages that utilize a question.

"Geez, you are ridiculously beautiful. Hello Zxena. my name is Eric, nice to meet you! I see you make music, what's your biggest inspiration? (This question references her mention of being a musician on her page.)

"Hello Liz. my name is Eric. I really like your face! I want to know everything about you, what do you do for a living?"

"Wow, it's almost strange how beautiful you are. Howdy Melissa, I'm Eric. What did you want to be when you were growing up? Did you become that person?"

Now let's take those same messages and instead of asking them a question, let's have a call to action. A call to action can come in the form of asking for a phone number or social media profile, asking them out on a date, and so on. Technically you're still asking them a question, but these specific questions require them to take an action versus just telling you about themselves.

"Geez, you are ridiculously beautiful. Hello Zxena, my name is Eric, nice to meet you! Five pictures just aren't cutting it for me, do you have an IG I can follow you and all your gorgeousness on?

"Hello Liz. my name is Eric. In addition to really liking your face, I am also a big fan of craft beer as well. Would you like to go to Goldstein's sometime? (This question references her mention of being "a craft beer connoisseur" on her profile.)

"Wow, it's almost strange how beautiful you are. Howdy Melissa, I'm Eric. I won't be able to put my phone down until I know two things, what makes you smile and your phone number. Please do share.

These are all some examples of first messages you can use to break the ice with your Tinder matches but be sure not to oversell yourself. Keep in mind, if you guys are together in a conversation on Tinder, this means she's showed interest in talking with you. Unlike on Instagram where you have to be more unique to cut through the noise, keep it simple on Tinder. Unless she is bored, most people actually go on Tinder to follow through and actually meet other people in person over dinner, drinks, hookups, etc.

Try to avoid having to deep of conversation in the Tinder app; you should honestly be trying to move the conversation into a text message within a few messages (no more than five), and from there, move the conversation into dinner within a few days. Getting to know someone through digital means (Tinder/texting/Instagram) is definitely a balancing act.

You want to communicate with them enough so not only do they want to meet you in person, but they also feel comfortable doing so. However, if you spend too much time messaging them and asking the fun, getting-to-know-you questions before meeting, it makes the date much more awkward because you have to spend time thinking about what you already know about them versus having fluid conversation and asking questions more freely.

Also, sometimes someone's texting personality is different than their in-person personality, and to be honest, the personality that really matters is the in-person one because that's who you're going to be spending time with. You don't want to text too much so that they formulate an opinion about your personality from texting; you want the first impression they have of you to be the one you make in person. This is why I suggest not spending too much time messaging back and forth, getting to know them. Instead, you should send a few messages back and forth to establish some connection and then make plans to see each other.

"I'd love to take you to dinner, are you available either Thursday or Friday?".

Make the proposal simple and straightforward. I only provided one example because I don't want you to overthink it. As I've mentioned before, never ask someone to hang out. Be specific; ask them along the lines of going out for dinner or drinks. In the same vein of being specific, don't ask them out in an open-ended manner. Ask them if they are free specific days this week. In all honesty, unless they are out of town, you shouldn't ever plan a date more than week out. The longer you plan it, the bigger chance of them bailing. Your sweet spot is planning a date one to three days out.

Chapter 5: The Old-Fashioned Way

As mentioned before, I've made my living starting and building technology companies or using technology to easily distribute my content. I've been a fan of technology my whole life. My father works in computers and got me into computers and technology at a young age. Although I've never learned how to create software/code because I've been on the business/sales side of technology, I've always had a huge admiration and respect for the way new technologies impact and better the lives of its users. I love it when technology disrupts human behavior and allows us to do more with less.

With that being said, I am still always a fan of doing it the old-fashioned way sometimes, heck, even most of the time as long as it works. Take shopping for example. Though I own an online store myself (smelldope.com in case you ever need to buy cologne), I still prefer navigating through traffic and fighting over parking spots at the mall so I can do my shopping inside a brick and mortar environment. For some reason, I love sifting through the racks and being able to feel and try on the clothing I'd like to buy.

When it comes to dating, I am still and always will be a proponent of doing it the old-fashioned way. I am at an age (turning 30 within six months of writing this) where I have been able to see this paradigm shift in dating. As I mentioned before, during the first half of my twenties I met people almost exclusively in-person. However, over the last four or five years, that ratio has definitely changed to about 50/50 when it comes to meeting people in person versus online. Also, even when I meet them in person now, the dynamic is different, and social media sometimes gets immersed in that in-person interaction.

In some sort, social media and dating apps have made meeting people in person a dying art. This should come as no surprise because as mentioned earlier, fear of rejection is the number one reason why people don't shoot their shot, even when they really want to. This is not exclusive to dating but pretty much anything in life; fear of failure/rejection prevents more people from achieving their dreams than failure itself. I hate to hit you with the cheesy Wayne Gretzky quote, but "You miss 100% of the shots you don't take."

Being rejected in person obviously hurts more than shooting your shot through digital means, which is the underlying truth of why many people solely rely on apps to date. That, in addition to the fact these apps have made many of us lose our social skills. However, if you remember the sales chapter, you should not fear rejection. You should embrace it and when you are rejected, smile it off and walk away politely.

Listen, it's completely alright to have a nervous knot in your stomach before approaching a complete stranger but don't let this fear debilitate you from potentially meeting your future partner. If you really want something in life, you need to go after it. Yes, if you're approaching a very beautiful girl, there is a good chance she gets approached by quite a few guys. However, as many guys approach her in person, there are 10x more guys sliding in her DMs. When you're able to meet someone in person, you greatly increase your chance of creating a connection with them compared to if you'd shot your shot through an app.

In-person, you have so many weapons at your disposal including your voice, pitch, body language, smile, and more. In sales, we always try to set up an in-person meeting with prospects who are considering buying our software. Yes, we do phone conference and video calls for those who can't accommodate an in-person meeting but when we are able to meet with them face to face in person, our chances of them signing up for our service increase by 50%. Never underestimate the power face-to-face interactions have.

So how do you go about actually meeting people the old-fashioned way? Well I'm glad you asked. We're going to break this down into two types of settings: natural settings and social settings. Natural settings are places people go naturally such as coffee shops and gyms. Social settings are places people go to interact with others but not necessarily strangers, such as bars, clubs, concerts, etc.

Natural settings

First, we'll go over the much harder setting to meet someone, which is in a natural setting where people don't normally go to interact with people such as the grocery store, gym, coffee shop, and so on. This is a much tougher atmosphere in which to meet someone because people are usually going to places like this to accomplish a task (eat, workout, etc.) and the last thing they are probably looking to do is meet a stranger. Because of this, you need to be very delicate about the way you approach someone in this setting.

First things first, remember you are approaching them unsolicited, so although you can come off as confident and direct, you don't want to come off too strong. Next, you don't want to take up too much of their time when approaching them; again, they are there to accomplish some task, so they may be turned off if you take up too much of their time. Lastly, always approach with a smile and excuse yourself with a smile, regardless of the outcome. Smiling will not only make them feel more at ease when being approached by a stranger but will help you look more confident when stepping up to bat.

<u>Coffee Shop</u>

Time to go over two natural setting scenarios and potential things you may say. Let's go with the most romantic traditional cliché setting, a coffee shop. You see a beautiful girl sitting alone reading a book two tables down from where you're currently working on your laptop. What's your move?

If you happen to recognize the book or know the author, you can lead into the conversation with that. If you don't know the book or author, don't try to fake it and lead with that because most women can smell bullshit and the worst first impression you want to make is talking about a subject you know nothing about. I use a book in this example, but in reality, this can be any common interest point you see such as her gym bag, college alumni sweatshirt, keychain, baseball cap, etc.

The book/common interest point is meant to be a lead you can use to break the ice and show there is some mutual interest, but you really don't want to talk about it for more than a minute. Once you've established dialogue, it's time to shoot your shot and transition the conversation to two simple but effective questions.

The first question you want to ask them is, *"Do you happen to be single?"* Before fully shooting your shot, you want to see if they are even available to date. Asking a girl if she is single helps you take less of a hit from the rejection bat if she is in a relationship/married versus if you go straight to asking them out. This simple question almost acts as a form of consent to ask them a follow-up question. This also gives the woman a less awkward chance to get out of the conversation and say she is in relationship, even if she isn't. If you do receive a no, it's always nice to say something along the lines of, *"Well he's a very lucky guy,"* then wish them a great day and let them get back to whatever task they were doing before your polite interruption.

Now let's transition to a more positive mindset and say that you asked her, *"Do you happen to be single?"* and she replied with a *"Yes"* and a big smile. The next step is simple, ask her out: *"That's what I was hoping to hear. Do you think I can take you to dinner sometime?"* or *"Great! I know you already have your coffee and book, but do you think we can grab coffee sometime later this week?"* If they say yes, then be sure to exchange numbers and go on your merry way. If you get to this point and they say no, wish them a great day and pat yourself on the back for shooting your shot at a stranger completely sober, that is, assuming you didn't pre-game before going to the coffee shop.

Taking a quick step back, what happens if you didn't have a common point of interest such as the book to break the ice with? Do you just walk up to them and say, *"Do you happen to be single?"* Kind of, but you're going to want to lead with an introduction and a compliment first. Let's say you really scanned for a common point of interest to break the ice but couldn't find anything. You can lead in/ask them if they are single with an introduction like below:

"Hello, (pause) sorry to interrupt you but I'm Eric, (pause) and I wouldn't have been able to forgive myself if I left here without at least saying hello because you are so beautiful (pause for a second, let her potentially say hello back) . . . *Do you happen to be single?*

Starting the conversation with the above example is obviously a much more direct way of shooting your shot versus looking for a common point of interest to break the ice with. Because it's much more direct, it's important to smile and speak slowly/pause because if she's looking down at her book or whatever activity she's doing at the moment, it may take a few seconds before you fully have her attention.

The Gym

For the second scenario of shooting your shot in a natural setting, I want to use the gym. The gym, much like a coffee shop, isn't a place individuals frequent in order to meet other people; it's where one goes to accomplish a specific task. So, just like the coffee shop, you need to be direct and very weary of dragging on the conversation and interrupting their workout.

For this specific scenario, let's say you are squatting on a smith machine (you should be squatting in a real squat rack) and she is dumbbell pressing on the bench next to you (no gender stereotypes over here). To make this scenario even more difficult, she has headphones on and looks very locked into her workout.

Before I go over how you should approach her, I'm going to start with how you SHOULDN'T approach her.

- First, you should never touch a woman unsolicited when approaching her. I'm bringing this up because you may think tapping her shoulder to get her attention is a good idea because she wouldn't hear you through the headphones, but you are wrong, and this is an easy way to get slapped.

- Next, you should never interrupt her during her set. Heck, you should probably avoid interrupting her right before or after the set either, as she's probably doing her best to focus on the upcoming lift and right after her set, she will probably be out of breath for the next few seconds.

- Lastly, unless you're a personal trainer or professional bodybuilder/powerlifter, you should never use critiquing her form as your opening line. Mansplaining is a terrible way to shoot your shot.

Now that we went over what you shouldn't do when approaching a woman at the gym, let's go over what you should do. Ok, first things first. Shooting your shot is easier if you're able to work out on a machine/ equipment next to the person you want to approach. Once you're able to work out next to them, try throwing out some feelers such as smiling to see if you're able to get any attention from them, if you don't get a smile back, no worries, they may just be super-focused on their workout. If you do get a smile back, you're about to make the next step easier.

You need to find the right time to talk to her. The less you're able to interrupt the workout, the better. You should ideally approach her about a minute after she's finished her last set. In this scenario she has headphones on. Ideally, you can wait for a moment when she takes off her headphones but if this moment never happens naturally, you're going to need to bring it to fruition yourself. The best way to do that is simply walk in front of her, smile, and wave hi to her; this should be enough of an indicator for her to take off her headphones to hear what you have to say. If she sees you wave and say hi but continues to keep her headphones on and look away, just cut your losses because this is her subtle way of saying she doesn't want to be bothered. Don't take it personal.

Once you fully have her attention, you're going to want to lead with apologizing for interrupting her workout. *"Hello, sorry for interrupting your workout . . ."* Once you get here, I have gone typically one or two directions: one leads to the phone number and the other their Instagram handle (safer route).

The first method is the more traditional compliment method; once you have her attention, let her know that you think she is very strong or you're impressed by her form/how much she is lifting. Do your best to avoid complimenting her body, even if it was a well-intended compliment; most of the time it will be received poorly. Once you are talking to her, you can transition the conversation to *"Do you happen to be single?"* and once you get there, you know what to do.

You: "Hey, sorry for interrupting your workout, but I wanted to tell you that you're a bad-ass. You have really great form."

Her: "Aww thanks, yeah, I'm always working on it."

You: "How long have you been lifting?"

Her: "About two years now."

You: "Well you look like you've been doing it a lifetime. I'm Eric by the way!"

Her: "Thanks, I'm Alexis."

You: "Well it's nice to meet you, Alexis, do you happen to be single? . . .

The other opener you can use, which I've had success with in the past (especially at the gym) is the *"You look very familiar"* line. The first time I used this opener, I was 100% honest in the fact that I thought I had met this girl before. I later realized we had never met before our conversation; however, we did end up talking and going on a date from this simple question.

The *"You look very familiar, have we met before?"* line has been around for ages and has been used by guys and girls since the inception of pick-up artistry. I'll be transparent, I'm a very honest person so part of me does feel bad teaching you a rather disingenuous opener, but it sure does work as a very efficient and easy-going way to start a conversation with a stranger.

My twist on, *"You look familiar,"* is to thread Instagram into the conversation. The 2018 version of *"You look familiar"* is *"Do I follow you on social media?"* Nowadays, you can know someone without ever having met them in person. Here is a potential way that you can open with "You look familiar" and seamlessly transition into getting their Instagram.

You: "Hey, sorry for interrupting your workout, but I wanted to tell you that you look super familiar as well as super pretty. Have we met before?"

Her: "(laughs) thanks, I don't think we have before."

You: "Ok, geez, you look so familiar, do I follow you on Instagram? You have an Instagram, right?"

Her: "I have an Instagram but I don't think we follow each other."

You: "Ok, well do you think I can follow you? I can't get over how pretty you are."

Her: "Yeah for sure, my handle is _____"

You: "Cool, I just followed you. I'll let you get back to the workout. I'm Eric by the way, it was a pleasure meeting you."

If you notice in this above example, you don't actually fully shoot your shot and go for the number or ask them out. There is a reason for this, and we'll cover it more in-depth in the next chapter, but understand that an Instagram handle is just as useful as a phone number. Also, you'll want to keep the conversation as short as possible in a setting like a gym; you don't want to end up irritating her and keeping her from finishing her workout. She will appreciate your directness and brevity with something straightforward like above. With this method, you can finish shooting your shot later in the DMs.

We've gone over two of the most formidable and nerve-racking places to meet a woman, the coffee shop and the gym. Although I used those two specific places in my natural setting scenarios, the same rules pretty much apply to meeting someone anywhere where people frequent, but typically don't go to meet others, including the grocery market, the library, the gas station, and so on. Remember, in all of these settings you are interrupting whatever they are in the process of doing, so be mindful and respectful about that when approaching them. And remember, always smile :)

Social Setting

Now that we went over the more difficult setting to meet women, let's talk about how to meet women in much more approachable social settings. A social setting is a place where people specifically go to socialize either with friends or new people they want to meet; the most common social settings are bars and clubs. However, if you're not a drinker, other social settings include concerts, bowling alleys, pool halls, etc. But keep in mind, just because women go to settings like this and socialize, don't think it's going to be walk in the park; there are a lot of things you need to keep in mind.

The two social settings we're going to cover are nightclubs and bars/lounges. What's the difference between a night club and a bar, you ask? Really the main difference is the fact that there is loud music and dancing at a nightclub and there typically isn't dancing at a bar, and if there is, there isn't a large dance floor space dedicated to it. With this scenario, we're going to solely focus on asking a girl to dance. If you don't know to dance, you should learn. Unfortunately, I'm not going to be able to teach you how to dance with a woman, but there are some useful YouTube videos for that. If you're the type of guy who doesn't even want to learn how to dance, you can skip to the bar game but please understand, dancing with a girl is definitely the easiest and most fun way to shoot your shot.

Night Club Game

Before we even start talking about what you should do while at the club, I want to caveat a few things upfront. First, if you're going to partake in the "pre-game" ritual of drinking before going to the club for that extra liquid courage, do your best not get sloppy drunk or, quite frankly, drunk at all. Your friends may be getting drunk, but you will have an unfair advantage over them because a) you'll have read this book and b) you'll have consumed less than them because you now have a natural confidence in your ability to talk to women. Next, even if you've only had one pre-game drink, just Uber to the club. This has nothing to do with shooting your shot; I just want my readers to be safe.

Ok, now you've Uber'd to the club, waited in line thirty minutes and payed the twenty-dollar cover to get in. What do you do next? I suggest grabbing one drink and making it last for a while. This is another reason I mentioned to avoid pre-gaming too hard; it's better to go into the club feeling good and enjoy your drink(s) there. Once you have your drink, take your time sipping it and just relax for a bit. Don't hang out on the dance floor until you're ready to ask girls to dance. Hang out near the bar or common area and simply enjoy the music playing, get in the zone. There is no need to rush this. The last thing you want to do is come off as eager and walk straight to the dance floor the second you get into the club.

So now you've been in the club for a minute, you're vibing to the music, and your cup is almost empty (you don't want to dance with a full cup); it's time to start shooting your shot. Unlike the other scenarios where there is more dialogue, asking a girl to dance is quite simple because all you have to do is exactly that, ask her *"Would you like to dance?"* I usually like to lead with a very brief compliment before asking but to be honest you don't have to say much more than:

"Hello, you're really beautiful, would you like to dance?"

In this case, it's less about what you have to say and more about how you approach them and your mannerism. Below are the Dos and Don'ts when dancing with a girl at the club, and as always, let's start with what not to do:

Don'ts:

- Linger/lurk on the dance floor. If you're going to be on the dance floor, you should be dancing, ideally with a girl or at the least your group of friends. A lot of dudes will just loom near girls who are dancing, seemingly in hopes of eventually touching or talking to them. It's really weird, and girls notice dudes who linger around too much. I typically hang out around the bar until I'm ready to ask a girl to dance.

- Dancing without asking. I know many of you have probably heard the terrible advice before that the best way to dance with a girl is to just walk up behind her and start grinding on her without asking. I'm letting you know now, this is terrible advice. I can't tell you how many guys I see at the club who will subtly dance behind girls, inching closer and closer in a hopeful manner until they are dancing "with" her.

- Approaching from behind. This is a very similar scenario to my last point, where you approach the girl from behind but at least this time you ask. Although this is a much better approach than just trying to grind on her unsolicited, you may startle her if you just ask her from behind. Ideally, you'd like to approach her from the front so that she can see you fully; however, I understand many times this can be difficult on a crowded dance floor. In that case, you can at least approach from the side; it's best if you come up to her and ask her while you're in her peripheral vision.

Dos:

- Approach confidently and with a smile. I know I've said it before a lot in this chapter but always approach a woman with a smile, in this case, a confident smile. In a natural setting like a coffee shop, you'll want to be confident but still approachable and conversational, and when it comes to a club, confidence is much more important. This is due to the fact that any given night at a club, a beautiful girl may get hit on a few dozen times; this is compared to the unlikely chance (zero to one) she is hit on each time she goes to the coffee shop. Smiling and asking her to dance with real conviction will help you stand out, compared to the guys who try to dance without asking or the ones who ask with a timid, shaky voice.

- Speak loudly and clearly. One of the best things about going to the club is the music they play; most of the time it's fun to dance and vibe to. At the same time, one of the worst things about going to the club is the music they play; it's usually super loud, making it very hard to hear someone standing a few feet in front of you. Because of this, it's important to speak loudly and clearly when approaching a girl. The last thing you want to do is ask her to dance with a low, quivering voice, and having her reply with "*What?*" forcing you to repeat yourself. Asking someone to dance only involves a few words, so take your time and make sure you pronounce each word correctly and loudly. Remember, your club voice is a lot different than your coffee shop voice.

- Balance dancing with small talk, the keyword here being *small*. Dancing with someone is a very great and intimate way to meet someone. However, if you can sprinkle in some chitchat, you can definitely make this first connection more personable. I specifically use the word "sprinkle" because remember, it's super loud in the club. So, you don't want to have a full conversation while dancing. I'd suggest maybe asking their name or a few other questions while dancing. You want to be efficient with your words. You should let your body movement do most of the talking but offering some light conversation while dancing will improve your chances of getting her number after.

- If it's a group of girls, it helps if you have well-enabled wingmen friends with you to approach and ask the girls to dance. Especially if it's only two friends dancing together, most girls don't want to be the one left out dancing in front of her friend alone. When you guys are dancing as a group, it helps women feel more comfortable. Understand that you don't always need a wingman and I've done plenty of solo missions, but it definitely helps.

So you've approached her respectfully and asked her to dance; she said yes and you guys have been dancing for a few songs. You definitely feel a connection, what do you do next? There are a couple of places you can take this, but let's start with the pessimistic (but still likely) scenario of her saying *"thank you"* for the dance and leaving.

You need to understand that most women don't go to clubs to meet men; most go to have some drinks and dance with their friends. This doesn't mean they're not open to dancing or meeting, but it just typically means that meeting guys isn't their priority when going to clubs. When she says she has to go to the bar or bathroom, this usually means she is excusing herself from dancing with you, but it doesn't mean she is not interested. She just wants to get back to enjoying the night with her friends. In this case, you should let her do exactly that, but you should do one thing before she walks away: shoot your shot.

Typically, when I am dancing with a girl and she excuses herself to go back to dancing with her friends or go to the bar or bathroom, I usually reply with something along the lines of:

"It was a pleasure meeting you. I think you're so damn gorgeous and I wouldn't be able to forgive myself if you left here without me asking for your number, may I have it?"

Even if she tells me that she's just going to go with her friend but come back and dance with me later, I'll still ask for her number on the off chance I don't see or dance with her again.

"Ok, I'll be ready to dance again but on the off chance I don't get to see you again, may I have your number? I wouldn't be able to forgive myself if I lost you without it."

In either of the above cases, once you get the number, don't talk to her again unless she approaches you the next time around. Even in the case where she says she will come back to dance again, she could have just been saying that as an opt-out from dancing with you again, which is completely fine because she was still interested enough to give you her number. If she really does want to dance with you again, she will initiate it.

Ok, what do you do when she excuses herself from dancing with you and you ask for her number, but she declines, saying, *"I'm sorry, I don't give out my number"*? Do you give up? Not quite yet; you have one more inquiry to make before throwing in the towel. Ask her:

"Ok, well may I follow you on Instagram?"

I can anecdotally tell you if a girl is interested enough to dance with you, there is a 50/50 chance she will give you her number after. However, if a girl is interested enough to dance with you, there a 95% chance she will let you follow her on Instagram. Most women (and men; I know I do) appreciate a new follower. Once you get the Instagram profile, you know exactly what do.

Don't take it personally if you ask for her number and she shoots you down but lets you follow her on Instagram. You're a stranger, and in case you turn out to be a creeper, it's easier to block/ignore you on Instagram than on the phone. Plus, you need to understand an Instagram handle is just as valuable as contact info, if not more so, than a phone number. If they are a little tipsy the night you met them, and you got their number, they may not remember who you are the next day or may be embarrassed of their behavior and not text you back. However, if you follow them on Instagram (and they follow you back), they'll remember you're the attractive, polite but direct guy that they danced with. Because of this, some guys won't even ask for numbers any more, but go straight for Instagram handles. I'm a little more old-fashioned and go for the number first, then the Instagram, but I'm happy to get at least one of these two pieces of contact info.

Now, let's go back to the scenario where you are dancing with the girl but here, she doesn't excuse herself. Well in this case, offer to buy her a drink or invite her to go talk on the patio/less noisy part of the club. Once you get to this point, just converse with her, make her laugh and feel beautiful. If she is still hanging out with you, she's definitely interested. Just remember to not walk away from that conversation without her number and/or Instagram.

Bar Game

This bar game portion will be shorter than the nightclub section because the nightclub section introduced a whole new element: dancing. And to be honest, having bar game is a lot like the coffee shop game, except there is alcohol involved. So, the bar game includes any place where people come to sit around a bar and have a drink, including lounges, restaurant bars, and the bar at the same club where you were scared to dance with girls and opted to work the bar instead.

The easiest way to meet girls at a bar, is to well, buy them a drink. I want to caveat one thing about buying drinks. **Buying a girl a drink is a gesture of good will, not a transaction.** Meaning, just because you buy a girl a drink, it doesn't mean she owes you a dance, a number, or even the pleasure of having a conversation. It's not uncommon for a girl to receive a drink and completely walk away after without thanking you. Although this is a little rude, there is nothing technically wrong with her doing this because you are simply using the drink as a gesture to show you are interested. Because of this, it's best to chat for a little bit before asking to buy her a drink. If you simply walk up to her and say *"Hey, do you want a drink?"* and the conversation ends there while you're getting the drink, there is a much greater chance of her leaving to talk to her friends the second you hand her the drink.

To increase the chances of getting to know her or at least getting her contact info after buying her a drink, it's best to introduce yourself and do your best to keep conversation flowing while you're waiting for the bartender to take your order/make your drink. As I've expressed in other chapters, introductions are always best paired with compliments. And in a bar setting, you definitely have room to come up with some funnier/unique compliments.

Below are some compliments + introductions + buying drink gestures you can use for inspiration:

"I just had to tell you that you're just darn beautiful. I could stare at you all night . . . I'm Eric, by the way, may I buy you a drink?"

"Hello, my name is Eric and I'd definitely swipe right on you . . . (she laughs) . . . Since we're not in the app, do you think I can just buy you a drink instead?"

"Sorry to bother you but I felt compelled to tell you have great facial bone structure, seriously, I'm crazy about your face . . . My name is Eric, may I buy you a drink?".

"Hey, my name is Eric and I've been mustering up the courage for the last hour to tell you that I can't get over how gorgeous you are. I really want to buy you a drink; can we please make that happen?"

"I really like your shoes, you have such a nice style . . . (a woman will always thank you when you compliment her style).. My name is Eric by the way, and I know started this conversation by talking about your shoes, but I promise I'm straight and I think you're really attractive. Can I buy you a drink?"

Ok, what do you do if she declines your offer? If she simply says *"no"* or *"I have a boyfriend,"* simply respond with, *"Well he is a very lucky guy"* and/or

"Have a great night." However, if she smiles and says, *"No thank you, I'm driving,"* or something along the lines of, *"Aww thanks but I had my last night for the drink,"* or perhaps says anything else that shows she's slightly interested but doesn't want a drink, smile and reply with the below:

"No problem, well if I can't buy you a drink, may I buy you dinner sometime?"

Every time I use the above question after my attempt to buy them a drink is negated, the reaction I usually receive from them is a smile and a bit of surprise. More than half the time, they will say *"sure"* and from there I will get their phone number or Instagram. Even if they decline the dinner offer, if I'm really attracted to them, I'll shoot one last shot. I usually tell them, *"Well it was worth a shot; may I follow you on Instagram?"* This is something I've done for the girls who have shot me down for a drink or dinner, but I thought they were so beautiful that I'd honestly be happy with a follow on Instagram and try my luck again down the road on there.

Lastly, if you're at a bar or club and you're not a good dancer and don't have the funds to offer a drink as a gesture, or you just don't want to wait at the bar, you can just use the above compliment examples I gave, but instead of asking them if you can buy them a drink, ask them if you can take them out sometime or simply just ask them for their Instagram. Below is one of the introductions + compliments we used earlier but with two different endings/asks:

"I just had to tell you that you're just darn beautiful. I could stare at you all night . . .. I'm Eric, Do you like food? (she says yes)/ Great, can I take you to dinner sometime?"

"I just had to tell you that you're just darn beautiful. I could stare at you all night but I know you'll eventually go home, so do you think I can follow you on Instagram so I can continue to admire you? I'm Eric by the way."

Chapter 6: Dating is also a lot like Marketing

In business, the two drivers of growth are sales and marketing. One of the more simpler definitions/ distinctions I can make for you between sales and marketing is this: Sales is the outbound process of you pursuing customers and marketing is the longer-term process of creating a brand and illustrating your potential value to customers so that they come to you to buy your product/service. In summary, sales is you going to the customer and marketing, the customer coming to you.

Although there is a distinction between sales and marketing, the majority of time you need to utilize both to close customers. For example, take a car dealership; someone may come to your dealership because they'd heard an ad (marketing) on the radio, but that person only became a customer once the sales guy or gal did their job correctly. Or another example of the opposite order is a gym employee who cold calls a prospect trying to sell them a membership; that prospect decides to hear the sales person out instead of hanging up like they normally do because they follow that gym's Instagram page for the great workout tips they post. In both scenarios, marketing and sales work together to turn these prospects into customers.

I covered sales earlier in the book and its relation to dating; now we're going to end the book on marketing and why exactly it is as important, if not more so, as sales when it comes to dating. First things first, you may not realize it but you've been learning about marketing the whole time. In both the Instagram and Tinder chapters, before I even taught you how to shoot your shot (sales), I taught you how to be marketable first by creating profiles the proper way.

Marketability

In the Instagram chapter, I stressed the importance of the leg work you should do before sliding in the DMs, which included following her profile, liking some photos, and doing your best to get a follow back. The main reason behind this is your ability to create awareness in her mind of who you are before messaging her. Creating this awareness will greatly increase your chances of getting a reply from her compared to if you message her out of the blue and she's never seen you in her life. This awareness you created for her is an awareness of who you are, which is what we like to call in business, your personal brand. Instagram is by far the most perfectly suited social platform for you to build your personal brand. This is why it's important to follow the dos and don'ts I shared in the Instagram chapter when it comes to your profile. Each photo and story you share is an example of your personal brand.

When it comes to Tinder, to be honest, it's all marketing. Unlike Instagram, you just can't send an unsolicited message to anyone you want on Tinder. There has to be mutual interest that comes in the form of them swiping right on your profile. Your Tinder profile is 100% marketing. With a handful of photos and a five-hundred-character-limit bio, you're doing your best to market yourself as a unique/funny/cool match. If you market yourself poorly, your lack of matches will reflect this. If you market yourself well on Tinder, well, let's just say you will have options.

Remember, marketability doesn't necessarily equate to being good looking. You can be a great-looking guy who gets very little matches on Tinder because you choose bad (non-marketable) photos of yourself and your bio, quite frankly, sucks and sounds bland and boring. Or on the other side of the token, you can be a very average-looking guy, but you get a ton of matches because you're doing fun and adventurous things in your photos and your bio makes all the girls laugh and swipe right on you. This is marketability.

The same logic regarding looks applies to Instagram as well; you don't have to be a male model to do well on Instagram. If you are a guy who consistently posts funny photos, videos, and captions and you're able to make your followers laugh, I promise, if you shoot your shot in a funny way, you will have some success. If you're an intelligent guy and you're consistently posting thought-provoking content, you will have some success sliding into DMs because girls will reply due to a genuine curiosity over learning more about your mind.

Lastly, when it comes to making yourself more marketable when shooting your shot in person, there are two very important actions you should take if you haven't already. One is easy but expensive and the other is cheaper but is much harder and time-consuming. Those two actions are dressing well and working out. I can't tell you how important these two aspects are to not only helping you meet women but just increasing your confidence in general and making you a healthier and happier person. I honestly feel bad that I'm bringing them up for the first time here in the final chapter but understand these two things have helped my game tremendously.

As mentioned in the preface (if anyone actually reads prefaces), I'm a pretty average guy; well, I was definitely much more average a few years ago. But what I mean is, I'm average height (5'8) and I'm not exceptionally naturally good looking, not bad looking, just a pretty average dude. Of course, now I have the title of CEO and published writer, which helps my game, but I didn't always have these assets at my disposal. In my early 20s, I always did well with women even though I didn't have money, height, or great looks. Because of what I lacked, I did my best to learn how to speak well, dress well, and build an attractive physique. I never became a bodybuilder by any means or a fashion model, but I did my best to learn how to excel above average in these areas and this greatly helped me with women. One important note: How you dress and how your body looks are variables you can easily control, so make sure they are helping your game not hurting it.

If you're already working out five or six days a week and you're already on top of your fashion game, then kudos to you. However, if you feel you lack confidence in either of these areas, you should make it a priority to improve yourself. I am not going to share with you tips on working out or becoming a better dresser, but I will point you in the right direction to some great resources, specifically some great YouTubers, because fashion and working out are both very visual things to learn.

When it comes to learning more about fitness and nutrition, check out these YouTube channels:

- YO ELLIOTT - STRENGTH CAMP
- Bodybuilding.com
- Jeff Nippard
- Christian Guzman
- Buff Dudes
- Scott Herman
- Fitness Blender

When it comes to learning more about fashion and grooming, check out these channels. I provided a variety from some that focus more on menswear and others that focus on streetwear.

- Teachingmensfashion
- Alpha M
- Alex Costa
- PAQ
- Harrison Nevel
- Richie Lee

The long game

In sales, you don't always close a deal on your first encounter with a prospect. Sometimes it takes weeks, months, or even years to do so. When you have a prospect who takes a meeting with you because they are interested in your product or service, but they decide not to buy what you're selling, it's usually for one of two reasons. The first is that they don't want to buy it because they don't see the value in it for them; the other reason they may pass is because they are not ready to buy it NOW.

For the prospects that fall into the latter category where timing is an issue, smart sales organizations will get these prospects onto some sort of email marketing campaign list. The intention of creating a list like this is to send an email every month or so to the prospects on the list, letting them know about new products, special pricing offers, or informational blog post. This type of email marketing is for those prospects who are not ready to buy the type of product or service you're offering at the moment, but when they are ready and in the market to purchase a product like yours, your brand will be in the forefront of their mind as a result of the monthly emails/reminders.

Let's give an example where you can put your feet in the shoes of a prospect. Let's say you are looking to sell your house and you decide to meet with two real estate agents from different real estate agencies about potentially selling your house. After chatting with them, you decide that you don't want to put your house on the market and use their services yet. One of the real estate agents thanks you for your time and gives you his card to hit him up in case you decide you want to sell your house in the future.

However, the other real estate agent goes a bit further. She thanks you for your time but also asks for your email address so that she can add you to her monthly newsletter. Over the next two years, you receive one email a month from her where she shares photos and stories of families she has been able to help sell or purchase a home. The photos and stories are very heartwarming, and you are genuinely happy to get one of her emails each month.

Fast forward two years. The combination of you receiving a very big promotion and having your second child have you ready to sell your current/first home and upgrade to a larger house better suited for a family. What real estate agent do you think you're going to call first to give the job? The one you'd met with two years ago whose name or face you can barely remember, never mind where you placed his business card? Or do you think you're going to reach out to the agent who'd managed to keep consistent awareness through the last two years via her monthly email newsletter. 99% of the time you're going to go with the latter.

This is a very effective technique sales teams use in business to help close deals. You start with sales to get your foot in the door with the prospect and let them know who you are; however, in the long-run it's the marketing and keeping your brand in the forefront of their mind that eventually closes the deal. In business, the biggest and best deals usually involve some combination of both sales and marketing to bring the deal to fruition.

Why am I bringing up this technique? Well, because it's something that you should be doing when you shoot your shot and it doesn't exactly swoosh. Specifically, for the times you shot your shot the old-fashioned way in person. In the majority of in-person scenarios I've shared during the last chapter, the goal of shooting your shot is to buy them a drink or get their number so you can take them out sometime. I mentioned in the case where they reject your attempts but show any interest at all, ask if you can follow them on Instagram. I also mentioned if they reject you because they have a boyfriend, tell them he's (or she) is very lucky and wish them a great night.

I mentioned you do these two things in the face of rejection for a specific reason. With the latter, it's just a polite and nice thing to say and many girls experience guys being rude to them after letting them know they are in a relationship. However, on top of that, you leave a great first impression that may come in handy later. For example, there was one time I was at a bar and I saw this really pretty girl with a cool Adidas hat on. I remember the first thing I told her was, "I really like your hat" and another compliment which made her smile; I then asked if I could buy her a drink. She replied she had a boyfriend, and I responded, "He is a super lucky guy" and told her it was a pleasure meeting her and wished her a great remainder of her night. A few months later, she saw me out at a bar and she had recently gotten out of that previous relationship. Although she and I only chatted for less than a minute a few months back, she remembered me and came up to say hi and ask me if I wanted a drink this time around. I not am telling you this story to convince you that you should be nice and polite to people because it may pay dividends later; I'm just saying you should be nice and act polite to people because it's the right thing to do and sometimes it will come back to you when you least expect it.

Now transitioning back to marketing and why I mentioned to always ask for the Instagram if they showed any interested but rejected your advances to dance, or buy them a drink, or so on. The reason I have you do this is because I want you to think of your Instagram profile as that one real estate agent's monthly email newsletter.

When you ask a girl out at the bar, she is making a quick judgement whether she wants to get to know you more based off your looks and the thirty-second conversation you guys had. In reality, she knows very little about you. If she is on the fence, she will probably say "no" to be on the safe side. However, if you're able to follow her and get her to follow you back on Instagram, you're letting her into your life a little more and giving her the opportunity to get to know the really cool person you are. Overtime you'll be able to build familiarity with her through your post and stories. She knows about your adorable dog named Miko; she sees when you go out of town with your buddies and have a good time; she sees you have a nice job with an office, and so on. She may even like and comment on your photos from time to time to let you know she remembers who you are.

So, if you do meet a girl out sometime and she passes on whatever your offer may be, ask to follow her on Instagram; you can definitely shoot your shot again down the road, but this time let it marinate before doing so. Instead of being all sales, let your marketing take over some of the workload. Let her follow you for a while and like a few photos before you shoot your shot again. There isn't a specific time frame I'd suggest waiting before sliding in her DMs, but a few weeks should suffice.

Also, if the content of your post is appealing enough aka your marketing is done very well, she may slide in your DMs. She may realize she would have actually liked to have gone on a date with you after getting to know you a little more as a bystander through your Instagram. However, remember, you're only going to get to this point if you market yourself well on Instagram.

Let's say in another scenario she followed you back, looked once at your profile which was full of mirror selfies, unflattering photos, and memes; it would probably give her validation for passing on your offer for a drink/date. Or in another scenario, she follows you after meeting you and takes a look at your profile which only has five photos since you only post once a year because you never post and build awareness; she will eventually forget who you are.

Closing Note

Listen, Instagram is a great app that you can use to meet people and market yourself but be cautious of getting lost in the sauce. Yes, I advise you should share on Instagram on a regular cadence if you'd like to meet people but don't obsess over this. Nor should you only share photos just for the sake of girls. You should be at a high level documenting your life, and your life's main pursuit should never be chasing women just as a woman's main pursuit should never be chasing men (or whatever an individual's preference is). Your main pursuit should be happiness, and although a partner can definitely play a big part in that, it should never be the sole catalyst of your happiness.

One of the most important things I can tell you is: Just be a good guy. Being a good guy doesn't mean you have to finish last or carry yourself like a feeble individual. A good guy just means you are a man of character. Always be direct and confident with your pursuits, but above all, you should be respectful to everyone. Even if a woman is rude to you in her rejection, brush it off with a smile and confidence; remember, you approached her unsolicited (most of the time) and so, you should never take rejection personally. And lastly, don't ever let fear or rejection prevent you from shooting your shot.

Acknowledgements

I wanted to first thank you again for reading my first book, I hope you enjoyed it and learned a thing or two. I'd also like to thank my friends Danny, Kyle, Josh and Anmmar for being my friends and allowing me to be a part of their acclimation to the single life after their very long relationships/marriages. I'd like to thank you my editor Richard Nicol for making this book much more readable. I'd like to thank you my ex-girlfriend Lex for helping me become a better man. Of course, I'd like to thank my family for always supporting me and my crazy endeavors. Lastly, I'd like to thank my management YBDR.

www.ingramcontent.com/pod-product-compliance
Lightning Source LLC
Chambersburg PA
CBHW070642030426
42337CB00020B/4126